Distinguished wealth Mindset:
Bridging the Gap between Rich and Poor Thinking

Michael B. Fuentes

Disclaimer:

The case studies provided in this book are based on real-life individuals and their journeys from a poor mindset to a wealth mindset. While these examples are widely known and have been documented in various sources, it's important to note that individual experiences may vary. The success stories mentioned are not meant to guarantee or predict any specific outcome for any individual. Achieving financial success involves a combination of factors, including personal circumstances, timing, market conditions, skills, and more.

The examples provided are intended to inspire and illustrate the potential for mindset shifts to positively impact one's life and financial trajectory. However, they should not be interpreted as a promise of instant success or a blueprint for achieving wealth. Real-world success is influenced by various external factors and the unique paths that individuals undertake.

It's advisable for individuals seeking financial improvement to conduct their own research, seek guidance from financial professionals, and consider their personal goals, risk tolerance, and resources. While mindset plays a crucial role, it's only one aspect of a broader strategy for achieving financial well-being. As circumstances can change over time, the experiences of the individuals mentioned may not be directly applicable to everyone's situation.

Table of content

Understanding Mindset Differences

Wealthy Mindset:

A wealthy mindset is characterized by an abundance oriented perspective. Individuals with this mindset tend to believe that opportunities are plentiful and that they have the ability to create and attract wealth. They exhibit several distinct psychological traits:

1. Abundance Mentality: Those with a wealthy mindset believe in the abundance of resources, opportunities, and possibilities. They view setbacks as temporary and are more likely to bounce back from failures.

2. Positive Self-Worth: People with a wealthy mindset generally possess a strong sense of self-worth and believe in their own

capabilities. They are confident in their abilities to navigate challenges and succeed.

3. Risk-Taking: Wealthy mindsets are comfortable with taking calculated risks. These individuals understand that growth often involves stepping out of their comfort zones and are more willing to invest time, effort, and resources in ventures that have potential.

4. Long-Term Vision: A wealthy mindset involves thinking beyond immediate gratification. Individuals with this mindset set long-term goals and are willing to delay short-term pleasures for greater future rewards.

5. Growth and Learning: People with a wealthy mindset value continuous learning and personal growth. They actively seek knowledge and look for ways to improve themselves, whether it's acquiring new skills or expanding their horizons.

Scarcity Mentality:

A scarcity mentality is rooted in a belief that resources are limited, and there's not enough to go around. Individuals with this mindset tend to focus on what they lack rather than what they have, leading to cognitive biases and behaviors that reinforce scarcity:

1. Limited View: Those with a scarcity mentality often perceive scarcity even when resources might be sufficient. This can lead to missed opportunities and a feeling of always being in a state of lack.

2. Fear of Risk: Scarcity mindsets tend to avoid risks due to a fear of potential loss. This fear can prevent individuals from pursuing new opportunities or making investments that could lead to growth.

3. Short-Term Focus: Individuals with a scarcity mentality often prioritize immediate needs and gains over long-term goals. This can result in decisions that provide short-term relief but hinder future progress.

4. Fixed Mindset: Scarcity mindsets might be associated with a fixed mindset, where individuals believe their abilities and circumstances are unchangeable. This can limit their willingness to develop new skills or pursue growth.

5. Comparison and Envy: People with a scarcity mentality might frequently compare themselves to others and feel envious of those they perceive as having more. This can lead to negative emotions and hinder self-esteem.

Understanding these disparities between wealthy and scarcity mindsets can be valuable for personal development. Recognizing the influence of these mindsets allows individuals to make conscious efforts to shift from a scarcity mentality to a wealth-oriented mindset. This shift involves reframing thoughts, building self-awareness, embracing change and challenges, and developing a proactive approach to pursuing opportunities.

Beliefs and Attitudes

Beliefs About Money:

1. Scarcity vs. Abundance: Individuals who believe in scarcity tend to view money as limited, leading to fear-driven decisions. Those who believe in abundance see money as a tool that can be multiplied through wise choices and investments.

2. Money as Evil vs. Money as Tool: Some see money as a source of corruption, while others view it as a means to achieve their goals and make a positive impact.

3. Deserving vs. Undeserving: Believing whether one deserves wealth can impact actions. Those who feel deserving are more likely to pursue opportunities and investments that can lead to financial growth.

Attitudes Towards Success:

1. Fixed vs. Growth Mindset: A fixed mindset believes success is based on innate abilities, leading to avoidance of challenges. A growth mindset sees success as achievable through effort, leading to a willingness to take on challenges.

2. Fear of Failure: Those who fear failure may avoid risks, missing potential opportunities for growth. Embracing failure as a learning experience encourages experimentation and innovation.

3. Locus of Control: Individuals with an internal locus of control believe they can influence outcomes, leading to proactive financial decisions. External locus of control may result in passivity and lack of initiative.

Perception of Opportunities:

1. Risk Perception: People with a negative outlook may focus on potential losses, while optimistic individuals see opportunities even in uncertain situations.

2. Timing: Believing that opportunities are time-sensitive can lead to hasty decisions. Patience allows for better evaluation of opportunities.

3. Networking and Relationships: Positive attitudes towards networking can open doors to valuable opportunities that might not otherwise be accessible.

4. Innovative Thinking: An open mindset promotes creativity in identifying and capitalizing on emerging opportunities.

Impact on Financial Outcomes:

1. Investment Decisions: Believing in one's ability to make informed investment decisions can lead to more successful ventures.

2. Income Potential: Attitudes towards one's ability to earn higher income can influence career choices and negotiation efforts.

3. Debt and Savings: Beliefs about debt (good vs. bad) and the importance of savings affect financial stability and wealth accumulation.

4. Entrepreneurship: Positive attitudes towards entrepreneurship can drive innovation and lead to the creation of successful businesses.

5. Delayed Gratification: A belief in delayed gratification can result in disciplined saving

and investing, leading to long-term financial security.

In summary, beliefs and attitudes create a psychological framework that guides an individual's financial behaviors. These beliefs influence risk tolerance, decision-making, and the ability to identify and seize opportunities. By understanding and reshaping these beliefs, individuals can change their approach to money, success, and opportunities, leading to more favorable financial outcomes and greater personal fulfillment.

Financial Education

Understanding Financial Literacy:

Financial literacy refers to having the knowledge and skills necessary to make informed and effective financial decisions. It encompasses understanding concepts such as budgeting, saving, investing, debt management, taxes, retirement planning, and more.

Importance of Financial Literacy:

1. Empowerment and Confidence: Financially literate individuals are empowered to take control of their financial lives. They have the confidence to make decisions that align with their goals and values.

2. Informed Decision-Making: Financial literacy enables individuals to make well-informed choices. They can assess the

pros and cons of various options and select the ones that best suit their circumstances.

3. Avoiding Financial Pitfalls: Understanding concepts like interest rates, credit scores, and investment risks helps people avoid falling into debt traps or making poor investment decisions.

4. Goal Achievement: Financial literacy facilitates effective goal setting and planning. People can map out their short-term and long-term goals and create strategies to achieve them.

5. Debt Management: Financially literate individuals understand the implications of different types of debt and can manage debt effectively, preventing excessive borrowing that could lead to financial distress.

6. Savings and Investments: Financial literacy helps individuals comprehend the importance of saving and investing. They

can identify suitable investment vehicles and strategies to grow their wealth over time.

7. Retirement Planning: Understanding retirement planning concepts allows people to start early and make the necessary contributions to secure a comfortable retirement.

8. Risk Management: Financial literacy includes recognizing various risks, such as inflation and market volatility, and employing strategies to mitigate these risks in investments and financial planning.

Impact on Money Management:

1. Budgeting: Financial literacy enables effective budgeting, where individuals allocate income to essentials, savings, investments, and discretionary spending.

2. Savings Culture: People with financial literacy prioritize saving a portion of their income, creating a safety net for emergencies and future goals.

3. Debt Reduction: Financially literate individuals understand strategies to pay off debt efficiently, reducing interest payments and improving overall financial health.

4. Responsible Credit Use: Financial literacy helps individuals use credit responsibly, maintaining good credit scores and accessing favorable loan terms.

Impact on Investment Management:

1. Risk and Return: Financial literacy allows individuals to evaluate investment opportunities based on risk and potential return, aligning with their risk tolerance and goals.

2.   Diversification: Understanding diversification reduces investment risk by spreading funds across different assets, industries, or geographic regions.

3. Long-Term Perspective: Financially literate investors focus on long-term goals, resisting the urge to make impulsive decisions based on short-term market fluctuations.

4. Avoiding Scams: Knowledge of investment basics helps individuals identify and avoid fraudulent schemes and investment scams.

In summary, financial literacy equips individuals with the skills and knowledge needed to navigate complex financial landscapes. It empowers them to make informed decisions, manage money effectively, and pursue investment opportunities aligned with their goals. Financial literacy is a crucial tool for achieving financial well-being, stability, and the ability to build and preserve wealth over time.

Risk-Taking and Innovation

Rich Mindset and Calculated Risks:

1. Comfort with Uncertainty: The rich tend to be more comfortable with uncertainty and ambiguity. They understand that risk is inherent in any endeavor and are willing to face it head-on.

2. Informed Decision-Making: Wealthy individuals thoroughly assess risks before making decisions. They gather information, analyze potential outcomes, and consider multiple scenarios.

3. Risk as an Opportunity: The rich often view calculated risks as opportunities for growth. They understand that high-reward opportunities often come with higher risks and are willing to take those chances.

4. Diversification: Wealthy individuals manage risk by diversifying their

investments. They spread their resources across various asset classes, reducing the impact of a single failure.

5. Learning from Failure: The rich understand that failure is a stepping stone to success. They learn from their mistakes, adapt their strategies, and continue forward.

Innovation and the Rich Mindset:

1. Openness to New Ideas: Wealthy individuals are more receptive to innovative ideas and technologies. They understand that innovation can lead to disruptive breakthroughs and substantial gains.

2. Continuous Learning: The rich prioritize continuous learning and self-improvement. They are willing to explore new concepts, adapt to changing market trends, and adopt innovative practices.

3. Entrepreneurial Spirit: Many wealthy individuals have an entrepreneurial spirit. They identify market gaps and are willing to invest resources in developing new products or services.

4. Calculated Experiments: Wealthy individuals are more likely to experiment with innovative approaches. They allocate resources for pilot projects or experiments to test new ideas before scaling up.

Poor Mindset and Avoidance of Risks:

1. Fear of Failure: Those with a poor mindset often fear failure and its consequences. This fear can lead to avoidance of risks and missed opportunities.

2. Loss Aversion: Individuals with a scarcity mentality focus more on potential losses than potential gains. They are hesitant to risk what they have, even if the potential rewards are substantial.

3. Short-Term Focus: A poor mindset can result in prioritizing short-term gains over long-term potential. This mindset leads to avoiding opportunities that might not yield immediate results.

Lack of Innovation and the Poor Mindset:

1. Resistance to Change: Those with a poor mindset may resist change and innovation due to a fear of the unknown or a belief that their current situation is the best they can achieve.

2. Limited Resources: People with a scarcity mentality might perceive themselves as having limited resources to invest in new ventures or innovative ideas.

3. Stagnation: A poor mindset can lead to complacency and a reluctance to adapt to

changing circumstances. This lack of innovation can hinder progress and growth.

In summary, the rich tend to embrace calculated risks and innovation because they approach opportunities with a growth-oriented mindset. They understand the potential rewards and are willing to take calculated chances to achieve them. On the other hand, those with a poor mindset often shy away from risks and innovation due to fear, a focus on immediate outcomes, and limited resources. These differences in mindset play a significant role in shaping the financial trajectories of individuals and their ability to seize opportunities for growth and success.

Goals and Vision

Setting Clear Financial Goals:

1. Direction and Focus: Clear financial goals provide a roadmap for individuals to follow. They give a sense of direction and purpose, guiding decisions and actions toward achieving specific outcomes.

2. Motivation: Goals act as motivators. When individuals have tangible objectives to work towards, they are more likely to stay committed and disciplined in their financial endeavors.

3. Measurement of Progress: Having defined goals allows individuals to track their progress. They can assess whether they are moving closer to their objectives and make adjustments as needed.

4. Prioritization: Clear goals help prioritize spending and saving decisions. People can

allocate resources to what matters most, avoiding unnecessary expenses.

Cultivating a Long-Term Vision:

1. Holistic Planning: A long-term vision involves considering various aspects of life beyond immediate financial needs. This holistic approach ensures that financial decisions align with personal values, aspirations, and life stages.

2. Resilience to Challenges: A long-term vision provides a buffer against short-term setbacks. Individuals are more likely to persevere through challenges when they have a broader perspective of their financial journey.

3. Delayed Gratification: A long-term vision encourages delayed gratification. Individuals are willing to forgo instant pleasures in favor of achieving greater rewards over time.

4. Wealth Accumulation: Cultivating a long-term vision often involves strategic wealth accumulation. It entails consistent saving, investing, and compounding growth over years or decades.

5. Risk Management: Long-term thinking involves planning for contingencies and managing risks that might arise in the future, such as healthcare expenses, job changes, or economic fluctuations.

6. Legacy Planning: A long-term vision extends beyond an individual's lifetime. It includes considerations for passing on wealth to future generations or contributing to charitable causes.

Synergy between Goals and Vision:

1. Alignment: Clear financial goals should align with the long-term vision. They contribute to the larger narrative of

achieving financial stability, growth, and the realization of aspirations.

2. Consistency: A long-term vision reinforces the consistency needed to pursue financial goals. It prevents short-term impulses from derailing progress.

3. Flexibility: While goals provide specifics, a long-term vision allows for flexibility in adjusting goals over time to adapt to changing circumstances.

4. Staying Grounded: Both goals and vision keep individuals grounded in their financial journey. They prevent distractions and keep focus on the bigger picture.

In summary, setting clear financial goals provides direction and purpose, while cultivating a long-term vision offers resilience, strategic planning, and alignment with personal values. Together, they create a framework for individuals to manage their finances effectively, make informed decisions, and work towards long-lasting wealth creation and financial stability.

Work Ethics and Entrepreneurship

Work Ethics:

Rich:
- The rich often have a strong work ethic that prioritizes productivity and effectiveness. They focus on high-impact tasks and delegate lower-value activities.
- They understand the importance of consistent effort and are willing to put in extra hours when necessary to achieve their goals.
- The rich are proactive in seeking opportunities for growth, and they are more likely to take on challenges and responsibilities willingly.

Poor:
- People with a poor work ethic might struggle with consistency, time

management, and completing tasks efficiently.
- There can be a tendency to procrastinate or to avoid tasks perceived as difficult or time-consuming.
- A poor work ethic might result in missed opportunities for career advancement or business growth due to a lack of dedication and effort.

Entrepreneurial Spirit:

Rich:
- The rich often possess an entrepreneurial spirit, seeking opportunities beyond traditional employment.
- They are more likely to take calculated risks to start new businesses or ventures and are open to innovation and creativity.
- An entrepreneurial spirit enables the rich to identify gaps in the market and develop innovative solutions to address them.

Poor:

- Those with a poor mindset may be risk-averse and hesitant to venture into entrepreneurship due to fear of failure or financial insecurity.
- There might be a lack of exposure to entrepreneurial concepts or limited access to resources for starting a business.
- A scarcity mindset can hinder the development of the creativity and innovation needed for successful entrepreneurship.

Willingness to Seize Business Opportunities:

Rich:
- The rich have a proactive approach to seizing business opportunities. They actively seek out and evaluate opportunities that align with their strengths and goals.
- They have the financial resources and networks to invest in new ventures or capitalize on emerging trends.

- The rich are more willing to invest time and money in learning new skills and expanding their knowledge to leverage opportunities.

Poor:
- People with a poor mindset might be more cautious and hesitant to seize business opportunities due to fear of failure or financial loss.
- Limited access to capital and resources can hinder their ability to invest in business opportunities even if they recognize them.
- A lack of confidence in their abilities or a scarcity mentality can hold them back from taking calculated risks and embracing new ventures.

In summary, the differences in work ethics, entrepreneurial spirit, and willingness to seize business opportunities between the rich and the poor stem from their mindsets, experiences, access to resources, and risk tolerance. The rich often exhibit a proactive and open approach, while the poor might struggle with factors that hinder their ability to fully embrace opportunities for financial growth and success.

Habits and Discipline

Habits and discipline are two fundamental pillars that play a pivotal role in shaping an individual's life, particularly in the context of financial success and stability. These concepts are interlinked, as habits often form the basis of one's discipline, and discipline reinforces the development and maintenance of positive habits. In this exploration, we will delve into the profound impact that habits and discipline have on financial well-being, discussing their definition, significance, and strategies for cultivating them.

Habits: The Building Blocks of Behavior

Habits are the routines and behaviors that individuals perform almost automatically, often without conscious thought. They are deeply ingrained patterns that shape our actions, decisions, and ultimately, our outcomes. In the realm of personal finance, habits can be constructive or detrimental, influencing how money is earned, spent, saved, and invested. These habits are not solely limited to financial transactions; they encompass the mindset and attitudes that guide one's financial choices.

Constructive financial habits include budgeting, saving, investing, and strategic spending. The act of budgeting involves allocating income to different categories, setting the foundation for a balanced financial plan. Saving becomes a habit when a portion of income is consistently set aside for future needs and emergencies. Investing habitually fosters the growth of wealth through compound interest over time. Strategic spending habits encourage individuals to make mindful purchases aligned with their financial goals and values.

Discipline: The Bridge to Consistency

While habits shape behavior, discipline provides the consistency required to maintain those habits. Discipline is the ability to exercise self-control, adhere to a plan, and resist impulses that may hinder progress. In the realm of personal finance, discipline serves as the bridge between setting intentions and achieving long-term financial objectives.

Discipline involves making deliberate choices that prioritize long-term gain over immediate gratification. It empowers individuals to resist the allure of unnecessary purchases, avoid impulsive spending, and stay focused on the bigger picture. Through discipline, individuals can channel their efforts into consistently following through on their established habits, even when faced with challenges or distractions.

Cultivating Constructive Habits and Discipline

Developing constructive financial habits and discipline requires deliberate effort and a commitment to change. Here are some strategies to foster these attributes:

1. Start Small: Begin with one or two manageable habits, such as tracking expenses or saving a specific percentage of income. Over time, these small steps accumulate into significant progress.

2. Consistency is Key: Repetition is essential for habit formation. Consistently practicing desired behaviors reinforces their automaticity.

3. Visualize Goals: Create a clear vision of your financial goals. Visualizing the outcomes you desire can strengthen your discipline and motivation to maintain habits.

4. Accountability: Share your financial objectives with a trusted friend or family member who can provide support and hold you accountable.

5. Eliminate Temptations: Minimize exposure to triggers that may lead to impulsive spending. Unsubscribe from promotional emails, unfollow shopping accounts on social media, and avoid unnecessary shopping environments.

6. Reward System: Reward yourself for reaching milestones and maintaining discipline. These rewards can act as positive reinforcement for your efforts.

7. Adaptability: Be prepared to adjust your habits and plans as your financial situation evolves. Flexibility is key to sustaining positive practices.

Habits and discipline are fundamental forces that determine an individual's financial trajectory. Constructive financial habits create a framework for wise money management, while discipline provides the consistency required to uphold those habits. By deliberately cultivating these attributes and integrating them into daily routines, individuals can navigate the complex landscape of personal finance with confidence and achieve long-term financial success and stability. Remember that the journey towards financial well-being is a gradual process, and each step taken in the direction of positive habits and discipline brings you closer to your financial aspirations.

Achieving financial success and stability is often the result of consistent daily habits, well-structured routines, and a strong sense of self-discipline. These practices empower individuals to make wise financial decisions, save diligently, invest strategically, and plan for the future. Let's delve into some of these key elements that contribute to financial well-being:

1. Budgeting and Planning: Establishing a budget is the cornerstone of financial stability. Regularly track income, expenses, and set financial goals. Allocate funds for essentials, such as housing, utilities, and groceries, as well as discretionary spending and savings. Creating a budget helps control overspending and provides a clear picture of where your money is going.

2. Automating Finances: Automating payments and savings ensures that bills are paid on time and a portion of your income is automatically transferred to savings or investment accounts. This prevents unnecessary late fees and encourages consistent saving habits.

3. Prioritizing Savings: Successful individuals prioritize saving a portion of

their income before addressing other expenses. Whether it's an emergency fund, retirement savings, or investments, setting aside money early ensures financial security and growth over time.

4. Educating Oneself: Continuously educate yourself about personal finance, investing, and money management. Books, podcasts, online courses, and seminars are valuable resources to expand your financial knowledge and make informed decisions.

5. Living Below Means: Avoid living beyond your means. Successful individuals make choices that align with their financial goals rather than succumbing to societal pressure to constantly upgrade their lifestyle.

6. Delayed Gratification: Practice delayed gratification by avoiding impulse purchases and instead saving up for items of value. This cultivates patience and prevents unnecessary debt.

7. Mindful Spending: Be mindful of discretionary spending. Prioritize needs over wants and evaluate purchases based on their long-term impact on your financial goals.

8. Debt Management: If you have debts, create a plan to manage and pay them off systematically. Start with high-interest debts and work your way down. Avoid taking on new debt unless necessary.

9. Investing Wisely: Invest according to your risk tolerance and financial goals. Diversify your investments across different asset classes to reduce risk. Regularly review and adjust your investment portfolio as needed.

10. Networking and Learning: Surround yourself with financially responsible individuals who can provide insights and support. Attend financial workshops or join

online communities to exchange ideas and stay motivated.

11. Setting Specific Goals: Establish short-term and long-term financial goals. Whether it's saving for a down payment on a house, starting a business, or retiring comfortably, having clear objectives keeps you focused and motivated.

12. Emergency Fund: Maintain an emergency fund that covers three to six months' worth of living expenses. This safety net protects you from unexpected financial setbacks.

13. Tax Planning: Understand your tax obligations and explore legal ways to minimize your tax liability. Utilize tax-advantaged accounts such as IRAs and 401(k)s to maximize your savings.

14. Regular Reviews: Periodically review your financial situation and goals. Adjust

your strategies as your circumstances change, such as getting a raise, starting a family, or nearing retirement.

15. Health and Well-being: Physical and mental health play a vital role in financial success. High medical expenses and reduced productivity due to health issues can impact your finances. Prioritize self-care to avoid such situations.

In summary, financial success and stability are built upon a foundation of disciplined habits and routines. By creating and sticking to a budget, automating finances, saving diligently, educating oneself, and making informed investment choices, individuals can navigate the path to financial prosperity. The key is to remain patient, persistent, and adaptable as you work towards your financial goals. Remember that small, consistent efforts over time can lead to significant long-term achievements.

Mindfulness and Gratitude

In a world often defined by its fast pace, constant demands, and material pursuits, the concepts of mindfulness and gratitude stand as powerful catalysts for reshaping our perspectives and fostering a sense of abundance. By practicing mindfulness and embracing gratitude, individuals can unlock a paradigm shift that attracts opportunities for growth, enhances well-being, and nurtures a profound connection with the richness of life itself.

Mindfulness: The Gateway to Present Awareness

Mindfulness, at its core, is the practice of being fully present in the current moment, without judgment or preconceived notions. It involves paying deliberate attention to our thoughts, emotions, bodily sensations, and the environment around us. In a world often characterized by multitasking and distractions, the practice of mindfulness allows individuals to break free from the grip of the past and the worries of the future, immersing themselves in the richness of the now.

When applied to the pursuit of abundance and growth, mindfulness becomes a tool for cultivating awareness of the resources, opportunities, and potential that surround us. By observing our thoughts and reactions, we can identify self-limiting beliefs and patterns that might hinder our progress. Mindfulness enables us to respond to challenges with clarity and intention, rather than reacting impulsively. As a result, we become attuned to the abundance that already exists in our lives—whether it's the simple joy of a sunrise, the support of loved ones, or the skills and talents we possess.

Gratitude: Elevating the Heart and Mind

Gratitude is a profound acknowledgment of the positive aspects of our lives, both big and small. It involves recognizing and appreciating the blessings we have, rather than dwelling on what is lacking. When we practice gratitude, we shift our focus from scarcity to abundance, from what we don't have to what we do have. This shift in perspective has a profound impact on our mental and emotional well-being.

In the context of attracting opportunities for growth, gratitude acts as a magnetic force that draws positivity and abundance towards us. When we radiate gratitude, we emit a vibration of contentment and positivity that resonates with others and with the universe. This positive energy can attract opportunities, connections, and experiences that align with our desires. Moreover, practicing gratitude reduces stress and anxiety, which in turn opens up mental space for creativity and problem-solving—key ingredients for personal and professional growth.

The Synergy of Mindfulness and Gratitude

The synergy between mindfulness and gratitude amplifies their individual effects, creating a dynamic and transformative cycle. Mindfulness helps us recognize the moments and blessings that often go unnoticed, while gratitude deepens our presence in those moments. The practice of mindfulness enhances our ability to experience gratitude authentically, as we become more attuned to the subtleties of life that inspire thankfulness.

As we engage in this cycle of mindfulness and gratitude, our perspective on abundance undergoes a profound transformation. We shift from a mindset of scarcity, where we focus on what is lacking or missing, to a mindset of abundance, where we acknowledge and appreciate the abundance that surrounds us. This shift isn't just a matter of positive thinking—it's a shift in perception that opens our eyes to the richness of experiences, relationships, and opportunities that were present all along.

Attracting Opportunities for Growth

When we operate from a mindset of abundance, our outlook on life becomes more expansive and receptive. We approach challenges as opportunities for learning and growth, and setbacks as temporary detours on the road to success. This outlook naturally attracts opportunities for personal and professional advancement, as others are drawn to our positive and resilient demeanor.

Furthermore, by embodying mindfulness and gratitude, we become more adaptable and open to change. We let go of rigid expectations and embrace the ebb and flow of life, recognizing that each moment is a chance to learn, evolve, and attract new possibilities. This flexibility and willingness to embrace uncertainty are hallmarks of individuals who invite growth and abundance into their lives.

In conclusion, the practices of mindfulness and gratitude are transformative tools that have the power to shift our perspectives towards abundance and attract opportunities for growth. By embracing mindfulness, we become keenly aware of the abundance already present in our lives and gain the clarity needed to navigate challenges. Practicing gratitude amplifies our positivity and creates a magnetic force that draws abundance towards us. When combined, these practices create a dynamic cycle that fosters a profound connection with the richness of life and opens doors to new opportunities for growth. As we cultivate mindfulness and gratitude, we embark on a journey of transformation that goes beyond material pursuits, enriching our lives with meaning, purpose, and an unwavering sense of abundance.

Overcoming Limiting Beliefs

Strategies to Overcome Self-Limiting Beliefs and Thought Patterns

The journey toward wealth accumulation is not solely determined by external factors; it is profoundly influenced by the beliefs and thought patterns that shape our perceptions and decisions. Self-limiting beliefs can act as invisible barriers, hindering progress and preventing individuals from realizing their full financial potential. To overcome these obstacles and unlock the path to wealth accumulation, it is essential to identify, challenge, and replace these beliefs with empowering thought patterns. This exploration delves into strategies to achieve just that, enabling individuals to break free from self-imposed limitations and embrace a mindset conducive to financial success.

Identifying Self-Limiting Beliefs: The First Step

Self-limiting beliefs are deeply ingrained notions about ourselves, our abilities, and the world around us that restrict our potential. They often emerge from past experiences, societal conditioning, or negative influences. Identifying these beliefs requires self-awareness and introspection. Here are some steps to help uncover self-limiting beliefs:

1. Self-Reflection: Spend time reflecting on your thoughts, attitudes, and reactions related to money, success, and wealth. Consider any recurring negative thoughts that surface.

2. Journaling: Write down any beliefs that come to mind when you contemplate wealth and success. This can help uncover patterns and underlying assumptions.

3. Triggers: Pay attention to situations or conversations that evoke strong emotions. These can provide insights into hidden beliefs.

4. Questioning Assumptions: Challenge assumptions that limit your possibilities. Ask yourself why you hold these beliefs and whether they are supported by evidence.

Strategies to Overcome Self-Limiting Beliefs:

1. Challenge Negative Thoughts: Once identified, challenge self-limiting beliefs by examining their validity. Are they based on facts or assumptions? Seek evidence that contradicts these beliefs.

2. Reframe Beliefs: Reframe self-limiting beliefs into positive and empowering statements. For instance, transform "I'm not good with money" into "I'm actively learning how to manage my finances effectively."

3. Replace with Empowering Affirmations: Create affirmations that counteract self-limiting beliefs. Repeat these affirmations daily to reinforce positive thought patterns.

4. Visualization: Imagine yourself achieving your financial goals. Visualization can rewire your brain and make the attainment of those goals seem more attainable.

5. Celebrate Small Wins: Acknowledge and celebrate your achievements, no matter how minor they may seem. This boosts confidence and dismantles feelings of inadequacy.

6. Seek Support: Surround yourself with individuals who uplift and encourage you. Engage in conversations that challenge negative beliefs and foster a growth mindset.

7. Educate Yourself: Knowledge is a powerful tool. Learn about personal finance, investments, and successful financial practices to boost your confidence and competence.

8. Practice Mindfulness: Mindfulness helps you become aware of negative thought patterns as they arise. This awareness empowers you to consciously choose more positive responses.

Cultivating Empowering Thought Patterns:

1. Abundance Mindset: Embrace an abundance mindset that believes there is enough wealth and success for everyone. Avoid comparisons and celebrate the achievements of others.

2. Growth Mindset: Adopt a growth mindset that views challenges and setbacks as opportunities for learning and

improvement. Embrace failures as stepping stones to success.

3. Self-Worth Separation: Separate your self-worth from your financial status. Recognize that your value as a person is not solely defined by your bank account.

4. Focus on Solutions: Shift your focus from problems to solutions. Instead of dwelling on limitations, channel your energy into finding creative ways to overcome obstacles.

5. Set Achievable Goals: Break down larger financial goals into smaller, achievable milestones. Each accomplishment reinforces your belief in your ability to succeed.

Consistency and Patience: The Key to Transformation

Overcoming self-limiting beliefs and thought patterns requires patience and consistent effort. These beliefs may have been with you for a long time, so be compassionate with yourself as you work to replace them with more empowering alternatives. Remember that change takes time, but with dedication and a commitment to personal growth, you can reshape your mindset and unleash your full potential for wealth accumulation. By identifying and challenging self-limiting beliefs, you pave the way for financial success and create a future defined by abundance and opportunity.

Networking and Relationships

Wealth Building Through Networking and Relationships:

In the landscape of financial growth and prosperity, networking, relationship-building, and leveraging social connections play pivotal roles in expanding one's financial prospects. The adage "It's not what you know, but who you know" holds true in many contexts, as the power of connections can open doors to opportunities, partnerships, and insights that may otherwise remain hidden. This exploration delves into the multifaceted role of networking and relationships in wealth expansion, highlighting strategies to harness their potential effectively.

The Network Effect: Expanding Horizons

Networking goes beyond the exchange of business cards at events; it's about creating and nurturing mutually beneficial relationships that can yield substantial returns. When individuals establish a robust network, they tap into a diverse pool of knowledge, expertise, and resources. Here's how networking contributes to expanding financial prospects:

1. Access to Opportunities: Networks expose individuals to a wide array of opportunities, from job openings and investment possibilities to collaborations and business ventures.

2. Information Flow: Networking facilitates the exchange of information and insights. Staying informed about industry trends and market shifts can aid in making informed financial decisions.

3. Collaborative Ventures: Partnering with individuals from diverse backgrounds can lead to innovative collaborations that spark new business ideas or investment strategies.

4. Support System: Networks provide emotional support, guidance, and mentorship from those who have walked similar financial paths. Learning from their experiences can prevent costly mistakes.

5. Referrals and Recommendations: A strong network can lead to referrals and recommendations, enhancing credibility and boosting one's chances of securing deals or clients.

6. Market Intelligence: By engaging with a broad range of professionals, individuals can gain insights into emerging markets, niches, and potential growth areas.

Strategies for Effective Networking:

1. Genuine Connections: Build authentic relationships founded on mutual respect and shared interests. People are more likely to engage if they sense sincerity.

2. Diverse Circles: Expand your network beyond your immediate industry. Cross-industry connections can bring fresh perspectives and opportunities.

3. Active Engagement: Attend networking events, conferences, and seminars. Be an active participant in conversations and discussions to establish your presence.

4. Online Platforms: Utilize social media platforms like LinkedIn to connect with professionals, share insights, and join relevant groups or forums.

5. Give Before You Receive: Offer assistance, knowledge, or introductions to others in

your network. This reciprocity builds trust and goodwill.

6. Follow Up: After initial interactions, follow up with connections to maintain relationships. Regular communication demonstrates your genuine interest.

The Power of Strong Relationships:

Building and nurturing strong relationships extends beyond networking events. It involves cultivating meaningful connections founded on trust, shared values, and mutual support. These relationships can yield significant financial benefits:

1. Partnerships: Establishing strong partnerships can lead to joint ventures, collaborations, and business growth. The collective strengths of partners can drive success.

2. Mentorship: Engaging with mentors or experienced individuals can provide invaluable insights, guidance, and shortcuts to achieving financial goals.

3. Strategic Alliances: Form alliances with like-minded individuals or businesses to leverage each other's strengths for mutual growth.

4. Access to Resources: Well-connected relationships can provide access to resources such as funding, expertise, and infrastructure.

5. Client Referrals: Strong relationships often lead to referrals, bringing in new clients and expanding your customer base.

Ethics and Authenticity: Cornerstones of Relationship-Building

While networking and relationships hold significant potential, ethical conduct and authenticity are paramount. Genuine connections are built on trust, transparency, and mutual respect. Here are some principles to uphold:

1. Honesty: Be transparent about your intentions and capabilities. Honesty fosters trust and credibility in your relationships.

2. Reciprocity: Embrace the spirit of give-and-take. Offer support, knowledge, and assistance without expecting immediate returns.

3. Respect Boundaries: Respect others' time and boundaries. Avoid being overly pushy or intrusive in your pursuit of connections.

4. Long-Term View: Focus on building lasting relationships rather than seeking quick wins. Long-term connections yield greater benefits over time.

Cultivating an Abundance Mindset:

Networking and relationship-building are enhanced when grounded in an abundance mindset. Embrace the belief that there are abundant opportunities, collaborations, and connections available for everyone. This mindset fosters collaboration over competition and encourages you to help others succeed as well.

In conclusion, networking, building relationships, and leveraging social connections are integral to expanding financial prospects. By strategically cultivating a diverse network, establishing meaningful relationships, and maintaining ethical conduct, individuals position themselves to unlock a world of opportunities, insights, and collaborations. The ability to connect, collaborate, and tap into the collective knowledge of one's network can lead to remarkable financial growth, while also enriching personal and professional journeys.

Investment Strategies

Wealth Mindset and Investment Strategies:

Investment approaches and strategies are fundamental components of achieving financial prosperity, especially when aligned with a wealth mindset. A wealth mindset involves cultivating an outlook of abundance, strategic thinking, and a willingness to take calculated risks to maximize financial growth. By adopting investment strategies that resonate with a wealth mindset, individuals can harness their potential to create, preserve, and multiply wealth. This exploration delves into various investment approaches and strategies that harmonize with a wealth mindset, empowering individuals to navigate the complex world of investments effectively.

Foundations of a Wealth Mindset:

A wealth mindset is grounded in several core principles that serve as a compass for investment decisions:

1. Long-Term Perspective: A wealth mindset embraces a long-term perspective, focusing on strategies that generate sustained growth and weather market fluctuations.

2. Strategic Risk-Taking: Calculated risks are viewed as opportunities for growth rather than obstacles. A wealth mindset encourages informed decisions while managing risk.

3. Diversification: Diversifying investments across various asset classes spreads risk and enhances the potential for consistent returns.

4. Continuous Learning: A wealth mindset thrives on knowledge. Individuals with this

mindset continuously educate themselves about financial markets, trends, and investment vehicles.

5. Adaptability: A wealth mindset acknowledges that markets evolve, requiring adaptable investment strategies to seize new opportunities.

Investment Approaches Aligning with a Wealth Mindset:

1. Passive Investing: This approach involves investing in funds or index-tracking exchange-traded funds (ETFs) that replicate the performance of a specific market index. Passive investing aligns with a wealth mindset by capitalizing on long-term market growth trends.

2. Dollar-Cost Averaging: Regularly investing a fixed amount regardless of market conditions, such as through monthly contributions to an investment account,

exemplifies the wealth mindset's focus on consistent, disciplined actions.

3. Value Investing: Value investors seek undervalued stocks with the potential for future growth. This approach resonates with the wealth mindset's emphasis on identifying opportunities that others might overlook.

4. Dividend Investing: Prioritizing investments in companies that pay dividends reflects the wealth mindset's goal of generating passive income and preserving capital over time.

5. Real Estate Investment: Investing in real estate properties aligns with a wealthy mindset's appreciation for tangible assets that can generate rental income and appreciate in value over the long term.

6. Entrepreneurial Investments: Investing in startups or businesses aligns with the wealth

mindset's willingness to take strategic risks and leverage expertise for potential high returns.

7. Alternative Investments: Including alternative assets like commodities, hedge funds, or private equity in a portfolio showcases a wealth mindset's openness to diverse opportunities beyond traditional investments.

Strategies for Embracing a Wealth Mindset in Investments:

1. Set Clear Goals: Define your financial goals and aspirations. A wealth mindset translates objectives into actionable investment strategies that align with your vision.

2. Research and Education: Continuously educate yourself about various investment options and market trends. A wealth

mindset values knowledge as a key driver of informed decisions.

3. Create a Diversified Portfolio: Diversification mitigates risk by spreading investments across different asset classes. This aligns with the wealth mindset's strategic approach to safeguarding and growing wealth.

4. Leverage Professional Advice: Consulting financial advisors or experts can provide valuable insights and strategies, reinforcing the wealth mindset's commitment to informed decisions.

5. Focus on Quality Over Quantity: The wealth mindset emphasizes quality investments with strong growth potential rather than chasing short-term gains.

6. Stay Disciplined: The wealth mindset encourages staying the course during

market fluctuations and avoiding impulsive decisions driven by short-term emotions.

7. Regular Review and Adjustment: Periodically reassess your investment portfolio and strategies to ensure they remain aligned with your evolving financial goals.

8. Embrace Patient Persistence: Adopt a patient approach that acknowledges that wealth accumulation takes time and commitment, aligning with the wealth mindset's long-term focus.

In conclusion, investment approaches and strategies that align with a wealth mindset are rooted in strategic thinking, long-term perspectives, and a proactive approach to financial growth. By embracing principles such as diversification, informed decision-making, and continuous learning, individuals can navigate the complex world of investments with confidence. A wealth mindset empowers individuals to make choices that lead to sustained prosperity, capitalize on opportunities, and contribute to their overall financial well-being.

Lifelong Learning

The Power of Continuous Learning and Personal Development in Navigating Changing Economic Landscapes

In a rapidly evolving world, where economic landscapes shift, technologies advance, and markets transform at an unprecedented pace, the importance of continuous learning and personal development cannot be overstated. These dynamic forces are not only essential for enhancing one's financial intelligence but also for adapting to the ever-changing economic environment. Embracing continuous learning is not just a choice; it's a necessity for individuals who seek to thrive and succeed in an era of constant change.

The Nature of Change: Adapting to Economic Shifts

The economic landscape is in a perpetual state of flux. Globalization, technological innovation, and geopolitical events constantly reshape markets and industries. Consider the rise of e-commerce, the advent of artificial intelligence, or the recent disruptions caused by the COVID-19 pandemic. These events have shown that those who possess the ability to adapt are better positioned to seize opportunities and overcome challenges.

The Role of Continuous Learning: Fueling Financial Intelligence

At the heart of adapting to economic shifts lies continuous learning—a proactive approach to acquiring new knowledge, skills, and insights throughout one's life. This pursuit not only enhances an individual's financial intelligence but also sharpens their ability to analyze trends, evaluate risks, and make informed decisions. Here's why continuous learning is a cornerstone of financial success in a changing world:

1. Staying Informed: Financial markets and trends are influenced by a multitude of factors. Continuous learning ensures that individuals remain well-informed about developments that impact their investments, savings, and financial decisions.

2. Navigating Complexity: Financial landscapes are becoming increasingly complex. Learning about various investment vehicles, tax strategies, and financial planning techniques equips individuals to navigate these complexities effectively.

3. Spotting Opportunities: Economic shifts often create new opportunities. By staying up-to-date with emerging industries and

innovative business models, individuals can position themselves to capitalize on these openings.

4. Managing Risks: Every investment carries risks. A solid understanding of risk management principles, which can be acquired through continuous learning, enables individuals to make more calculated decisions.

5. Adapting Investment Strategies: Different economic climates call for different investment strategies. Learning about diverse approaches, from conservative to aggressive, empowers individuals to adjust their tactics as needed.

Embracing Personal Development: Building Resilience

Personal development complements continuous learning by cultivating the mindset and skills necessary to navigate change with resilience and adaptability. The ability to embrace uncertainty, communicate effectively, and manage stress contributes significantly to one's capacity to thrive in shifting economic landscapes.

1. Emotional Intelligence: Personal development nurtures emotional intelligence—the ability to understand and manage emotions. This skill is crucial for making rational decisions during market fluctuations and economic uncertainty.

2. Communication Skills: Effective communication is vital in business and finance. Personal development hones skills like negotiation, networking, and public speaking, enhancing an individual's ability to connect and collaborate.

3. Critical Thinking: Developing critical thinking skills empowers individuals to evaluate information, analyze situations, and make reasoned decisions—a valuable

trait when faced with complex financial choices.

4. Resilience and Adaptability: Personal development fosters resilience—the ability to bounce back from setbacks—and adaptability—the capacity to thrive in changing circumstances. These qualities are indispensable in uncertain economic environments.

A Mindset of Lifelong Learning: Cultivating Curiosity

Cultivating a mindset of lifelong learning and personal development is a transformative journey that requires dedication and curiosity. Here's how to embrace these principles effectively:

1. Set Learning Goals: Define specific learning goals related to finance, business, or personal growth. These goals provide

direction and purpose to your learning journey.

2. Diversify Your Learning Sources: Explore a variety of learning resources, including books, online courses, workshops, seminars, and podcasts. This diverse approach enriches your perspectives.

3. Network and Collaborate: Engage with peers, mentors, and experts in your field. Their insights and experiences can offer valuable lessons and perspectives.

4. Experiment and Apply: Apply your newfound knowledge in real-life scenarios. Experimentation fosters experiential learning and enhances your ability to adapt.

5. Stay Open-Minded: Embrace curiosity and a willingness to challenge your existing beliefs. This open-minded approach fosters growth and innovation.

The Continuous Learning Advantage: A Lifelong Investment

In a world where economic landscapes are in constant flux, continuous learning and personal development are investments with unparalleled returns. They empower individuals to develop financial acumen, adapt to change, and thrive in uncertainty. By staying informed, honing skills, and cultivating a resilient mindset, individuals not only enhance their financial intelligence but also position themselves as confident and agile participants in an ever-changing economic ecosystem. In essence, the pursuit of continuous learning and personal development is a lifelong journey that unlocks opportunities, fuels growth, and ensures that individuals remain at the forefront of success, no matter how the economic winds may shift.

Generosity and Giving Back

The Synergy of Charitable Giving and the Wealth Mindset:

In the pursuit of wealth and financial prosperity, there exists a profound paradox: the more we give, the more we receive. Charitable giving and contributing to the community are not just noble acts; they align seamlessly with a wealth mindset and have the power to lead to a more fulfilling and impactful life. The synergy between generosity and prosperity lies in the recognition that true wealth transcends monetary gains and resides in the positive influence we have on the lives of others and the communities we touch.

Redefining Wealth: Beyond Material Accumulation

A wealth mindset extends beyond the accumulation of material possessions; it encompasses a holistic perspective that values abundance in all aspects of life. This includes relationships, personal growth, and the ability to make a positive impact on the world. By embracing charitable giving and community contribution, individuals can redefine their understanding of wealth, recognizing that true prosperity is found in the well-being of oneself and the greater community.

The Fulfillment of Generosity: A Deeper Sense of Purpose

At the heart of the wealth mindset is the recognition that wealth is a tool that can be leveraged for the betterment of others. Charitable giving provides individuals with the opportunity to create a meaningful legacy and contribute to causes that align with their values. When we give, we experience a sense of fulfillment and purpose that transcends the temporary satisfaction of material acquisitions. This fulfillment arises from the knowledge that our actions are making a tangible difference in the lives of others.

Impactful Living Through Giving:

1. Enhanced Well-Being: Studies have shown that giving to others is linked to increased well-being and happiness. The act of contributing to the community fosters a sense of connectedness and purpose that enriches our own lives.

2. Positive Ripple Effect: Charitable acts have a ripple effect that extends beyond the immediate recipient. By improving the lives of individuals or communities, we set in motion a chain of positivity that can lead to broader societal transformation.

3. Stronger Communities: Contributing to the community strengthens its fabric. Whether it's supporting educational programs, healthcare initiatives, or social

services, our efforts contribute to creating a healthier, more vibrant community.

4. Inspiring Change: Charitable giving can inspire others to take action. Our generosity serves as a model for those around us, encouraging them to also contribute and make a positive impact.

The Wealth Mindset in Action: A Harmonious Partnership

Charitable giving and the wealth mindset are not opposing forces; rather, they form a harmonious partnership that enables individuals to lead more fulfilling and impactful lives. Here's how they work in tandem:

1. Strategic Philanthropy: The wealth mindset's strategic approach extends to philanthropy. Just as individuals allocate resources to investments, they can allocate

resources to charitable causes that align with their passions and values.

2. Maximizing Resources: The wealth mindset emphasizes efficiency and value creation. When applied to charitable giving, this means finding ways to maximize the impact of each dollar donated, ensuring it reaches those who need it most.

3. Long-Term Vision: Just as the wealth mindset takes a long-term view of financial growth, charitable giving focuses on creating lasting, sustainable change. Investments in education, healthcare, and social programs can have far-reaching effects that endure over time.

4. Collaboration and Innovation: The wealth mindset's openness to collaboration and innovation extends to philanthropy. Individuals can leverage their networks, resources, and expertise to drive innovative solutions to societal challenges.

Practical Ways to Align Charitable Giving with a Wealth Mindset:

1. Set Giving Goals: Just as financial goals are set for wealth accumulation, establish giving goals that reflect the causes you're passionate about.

2. Research and Due Diligence: Apply the same diligence to charitable organizations as you would to investment opportunities. Research their impact, transparency, and financial stewardship.

3. Strategic Involvement: Just as the wealth mindset emphasizes strategic investments, consider actively engaging with organizations through volunteering, mentorship, or advisory roles.

4. Measurement of Impact: Evaluate the impact of your charitable contributions by measuring the tangible outcomes they

generate. This aligns with the wealth mindset's focus on results.

Conclusion: A Legacy of Prosperity and Impact

In merging the concepts of charitable giving and the wealth mindset, individuals have the opportunity to leave a legacy that transcends financial prosperity. By recognizing the interconnectedness of wealth, well-being, and community, individuals can harness the power of their resources to enrich lives, foster positive change, and create a lasting impact. Through strategic philanthropy, collaboration, and a commitment to making a difference, individuals can transform their pursuit of wealth into a journey of purpose, fulfillment, and meaningful contribution to the greater good. Ultimately, it's a partnership that underscores the profound truth that in giving, we truly receive.

Case Studies and Success Stories

Real-life examples of individuals who transitioned from a poor mindset to a wealth mindset and achieved financial success:

1. Oprah Winfrey: Oprah Winfrey grew up in poverty and faced numerous challenges in her early life. However, she had a strong determination to succeed and believed in her potential. Through hard work and a persistent mindset, Oprah transitioned from a difficult upbringing to become one of the most influential media moguls in the world. She built a media empire, including her own talk show, magazine, production company, and network. Oprah's success can be attributed to her focus on personal growth, continuous learning, and the belief that she could create her own destiny.

2. Chris Gardner: Chris Gardner's life story was portrayed in the movie "The Pursuit of Happiness." He went from being homeless and struggling to make ends meet to becoming a successful stockbroker and entrepreneur. Gardner's journey was marked by perseverance, resilience, and a strong determination to provide a better life for his son. Despite facing numerous setbacks, he refused to give up and eventually secured a job at a prestigious brokerage firm. His story exemplifies the power of a positive mindset, hard work, and the refusal to let circumstances define one's future.

3. Warren Buffett: Warren Buffett, often referred to as the "Oracle of Omaha," is one of the world's wealthiest individuals. However, he didn't start out with a silver spoon. Early in life, he displayed an entrepreneurial spirit, selling newspapers and golf balls to earn money. Buffett's wealth mindset was shaped by his voracious

appetite for learning and his ability to see opportunities where others saw challenges. He developed a disciplined approach to investing, focusing on long-term value and avoiding impulsive decisions. His journey from modest beginnings to becoming a renowned investor and philanthropist is a testament to his transformational mindset.

4. Robert Kiyosaki: Robert Kiyosaki, the author of "Rich Dad Poor Dad," was once in a financially challenging situation himself. He came from a middle-class background and realized that traditional education didn't teach him about money and wealth-building. Kiyosaki's perspective shifted when he started learning from his friend's "rich dad," who taught him valuable lessons about investing, assets, and passive income. Kiyosaki embraced the idea of acquiring assets that generate income, rather than relying solely on earned income from a job. Through his books, seminars, and real estate investments, he empowered

countless individuals to change their mindset about money and achieve financial independence.

In each of these cases, the transition from a poor mindset to a wealth mindset involved a combination of factors: unwavering determination, a willingness to learn and adapt, embracing opportunities, and a belief in one's capacity to overcome challenges. These individuals used their experiences and hardships as catalysts for personal growth and financial success, demonstrating that a shift in mindset can truly transform lives.

Going forward, here are two more case studies of individuals who shifted from a poor mindset to a wealth mindset and achieved financial success:

5. Daymond John: Daymond John is best known as one of the "sharks" on the TV show "Shark Tank." He grew up in a

working-class family and faced challenges such as dyslexia. Despite his struggles, John developed a strong work ethic and a knack for entrepreneurship from a young age. He founded the clothing brand FUBU (For Us By Us) with a few friends, starting by sewing hats in his mother's house. Through determination, creative marketing, and leveraging connections, FUBU eventually grew into a multimillion-dollar fashion brand. Daymond John's journey showcases how embracing your unique strengths, leveraging networks, and persevering through obstacles can lead to remarkable success.

6. J.K. Rowling: Before becoming a household name with the "Harry Potter" series, J.K. Rowling faced her share of challenges. She was a struggling single mother living on welfare and battling depression. Despite her difficult circumstances, Rowling had a wealth of imagination and a passion for writing. She

channeled her creativity into creating the magical world of Harry Potter. After numerous rejections from publishers, she finally secured a book deal. Rowling's story underscores the importance of resilience, self-belief, and the transformative power of using adversity as a stepping stone toward success. Her journey from poverty to becoming one of the world's wealthiest authors is an inspiration to aspiring writers and entrepreneurs alike.

These additional case studies emphasize that a shift from a poor mindset to a wealth mindset involves recognizing one's unique strengths, harnessing creativity, and pushing through challenges. Each individual demonstrated an unwavering commitment to their goals, a willingness to learn and adapt, and the ability to seize opportunities even in the face of adversity. Their stories serve as reminders that anyone, regardless of their starting point, can achieve financial success by cultivating the right mindset and taking consistent action toward their dreams.